In the Path of the
GRIZZLY

In the Path of the GRIZZLY

Text and Photography by Alan Carey

NORTHLAND PRESS ❁ FLAGSTAFF, ARIZONA

Frontispiece: The grizzly, scientifically designated *Ursus arctos horribilis,* is considered a brown bear. Other than size, there is very little difference between grizzlies and the brown bears that roam coastal Alaska. The average weight of an adult grizzly ranges from between three hundred fifty to six hundred pounds; very rarely, they will reach a thousand pounds. Not a particularly social creature, the grizzly requires a range of about twenty to one thousand square miles.

To Ginny

Contents

Symbol of the Wilderness   3

A Personal Perspective   7

Profile of a Grizzly   23

The Lighter Side of the Grizzly   41

Bear Versus Man   55

Will the Grizzly Survive?   65

Acknowledgements

Without the assistance and support of a number of people, this book would not have been possible.

First of all, I would like to thank Lance Olsen, president of the Great Bear Foundation, for taking the time to read over the final draft and offer suggestions and comments on the text that proved invaluable. Also, I am indebted to Chuck Jonkel, head of the Border Grizzly Project, and John Craighead and Jay Sumner of the Wildlife-Wildlands Institute; they all provided important biological information on the grizzly. I would also like to express my appreciation to those individuals who took the time to relate their personal experiences to me, some of which are included in this book.

Last, but certainly not least, I owe a special thanks to two charming ladies. One is my good friend, Barbara Gates, who offered me her writing talents and proved to be so helpful in assembling this text. The other is my wife Ginny; her exceptional typing skills and her endless patience were invaluable. She endured my absenses from home while I was following the path of the grizzly. It was her strong support that allowed me to complete this work.

Symbol
of the Wilderness

Through the years, man has carved out huge chunks of the western North American wilderness for his own needs. Despite this, it still remains some of the most magnificent landscape on earth. From the mudpots of Yellowstone to the northern tundra at the foot of Mt. McKinley, the land of the grizzly is vast and beautiful. It is a landscape dominated by towering snowcapped peaks that pierce the clouds. Glaciers cling to these high mountains, sending sparkling streams cascading down to rocky basins, and finally, into emerald-green lakes.

When a grizzly stands, it is usually to get a better look—not, as some believe, in preparation for an attack.

In the spring and summer, lush alpine meadows are adorned with a rich tapestry of paintbrush, beargrass, shooting stars, lilies, and scores of other wildflowers. Thick forests of spruce, lodgepole, and Douglas fir flank the mountain's slopes and clothe the lower valleys. In autumn, golden quaking aspen leaves shimmer in the wind. Farther north, the dwarf birch, willow, blueberry, and bearberry decorate the vast tundra with shades of yellow, orange, and red.

Winter brings snow and arctic air that is made more intense by gale-force winds. A hush hangs over the land, a stillness almost unnatural to the ears.

The wilderness is this and much more. To describe wilderness only in terms of beautiful scenery, however, is the same as limiting a description of one's home solely to the outer walls. The wilderness and the home are not shallow, one-dimensional shells, but rather, places that support life.

Along the length of the great western wilderness areas, herds of caribou still migrate across the tundra. Mountain goats, bighorn, and Dall sheep cling to cliffs on treeless mountain tops. The bugle of the elk breaks the quiet of a late September sunset. Moose and beaver feed in willow-fringed ponds. The lynx hunts snowshoe hare within dense stands of spruce, while packs of wolves can be heard howling on a moonlit night. And, yes, the grizzly still ambles across high mountain meadows, with a destination known only to himself.

All of these are good representatives of the wilderness, but none quite compare with the grizzly. This great bear seems almost as rugged and awe-inspiring as the mountainous, snowcovered terrain in which he lives.

He possesses extraordinary strength that enables him to drag an eight-hundred pound elk with no apparent effort. His stamina carries him up mountain slopes at a fast, ground-eating gait, and yet, he is agile enough to turn on a dime at full throttle. Highly intelligent, this great animal seems to have the ability to reason.

When a big silvertip grizzly lopes across an alpine meadow in long power-driven strides, heavy muscles rippling with each bound, massive head swinging from side to side, he is an awesome sight. His very presence commands respect from all living things. Is there any other that serves as a better symbol of the true wilderness than the grizzly?

Yet, as we watch this symbol of nature's power disappear over the next rise, we might ask of ourselves, "Where is the grizzly headed? What obstacles will he encounter? Where does his destiny lie?" Within these questions we find a common bond of concern between the great bear—the grizzly—and another of nature's more powerful beings: man. The bond is that of survival.

Grizzlies prefer the wilderness, land where human impact is minimal; this mountainous country in Glacier National Park fulfills that requirement.

A Personal Perspective

This is a very personal account of one wildlife photographer's ongoing fascination with the grizzly. There are numerous, very significant, and scientifically based studies that have been made and published on this animal, and my intent is to complement them. For a photographer, few animals offer such potential for dramatic pictures as does the grizzly; the challenge is not to be discounted, either.

My fascination with the grizzly goes back quite a few years to my Michigan childhood. When I was about ten, my brother-in-law gave me stacks of *Field & Stream* and *Outdoor Life* that he had collected over

A mountain grizzly runs against a strong autumn wind.

the years; the first thing I did was thumb through them until I came to one that had a photo or painting of a ferocious grizzly on the cover. He would have bared teeth, great claws, and would be charging a hunter or barreling into a campsite in the middle of the night, terrorizing its occupants. The stories inside the magazines documented how the hunters had killed the charging grizzly when it was within fifteen feet, using their final bullet. I remember other accounts in which a hunter or fisherman surprised a grizzly and was unfortunate enough to be attacked or seriously mauled; more often than not, the graphic descriptions made me excitedly squeamish.

Although these stories produced a shiver of fear at the prospect of meeting a grizzly, it also sparked an interest that eventually was a contributing factor in my decision to move to Wyoming, then finally to Montana, which is presently my home. Somehow, I felt the need to live in those places that I had only read about.

The beauty of the land and its inhabitants inspired me to take up photography, first as a hobby, then as a profession. Though I delighted in capturing on film the great variety of animals that lived in the area, the grizzly always symbolized something almost mystical to me. It was a short time after I moved to Montana that I had my first experience with the grizzly. It was on a spring morning in Yellowstone National Park. Ten years have passed, but I will long remember the events of that day.

Starting to feel the strain of climbing the steep ridge, I pushed ahead at a demanding pace high above the Lamar River in Yellowstone National Park. The early morning sun was beginning to melt the frost covering the thigh-deep grass. It was the end of May, and spring had finally come to this high-altitude park.

Just ahead of me was a large grove of quaking aspen and about fifty yards beyond, in an open meadow, was a herd of sixty elk. I had first spied the elk from the valley floor, and was certain that they would still be feeding in the same place when I arrived. As I entered the stand of aspen, I slowed down, moving carefully so as not to betray my presence to the elk. Almost tiptoeing through the timber, I saw something that froze me in midstep. Directly ahead, imprinted in the damp earth, were the unmistakable tracks of the great bear, the grizzly. They were very sharp and very fresh. The long claws had broken the dirt almost two inches from the pad marks.

The effect was unnerving. The only thing I could hear was the thumping of my heart; I strained my eyes, searching the surrounding trees for movement, a dark silhouette, anything that would give away the bear's location. My ears were attuned to the sound of footsteps or an ominous growl.

Suddenly, I heard a twig snap. Far ahead, at the edge of the timber, I caught a glimpse of movement. My nerves were stretched to the limit. All those magazine covers came rushing back to my mind: the teeth, the mauled hunters, the terror of all the accounts I had consumed so long ago. (I could see myself as the subject of an article at that point.) But curiosity was stronger than fear. I stepped slightly to the left, for a better look through the expanse of trees. That action provoked a loud snort, followed by a tremendous crashing of brush. I was ready to panic when, through an open lane in the thick timber, I saw the cause of all the commotion. The elk herd was tearing down the flank of the mountain.

I watched and listened as the sound of thundering hooves rapidly dissolved and the air was once again filled by almost perfect stillness. Evidently, the elk had begun moving into the timber and either heard or scented me, then fled. My composure had

A silvertip grizzly, called Real Bear by the Blackfoot Indians

9

been badly shaken, but I began to recover; my heartbeat returned to a more normal rate. I was relieved and at the same time, disappointed, at not seeing the grizzly, but the disappointment was lessened by the knowledge that he had been here. Below me were his tracks, evidence of his passing sometime during the night or in the morning hours. He was out there . . . somewhere. The thought was strong: "We'll meet someday, my friend." And we have.

Through the viewfinder of my camera, I have witnessed the grizzly in all his moods—from lighthearted playfulness to violent rage. He has provided me with some laughs, but has also made a contribution to my thinning hair. I doubt whether he has enjoyed my company as much as I've enjoyed his. Nevertheless, for me, each experience has been nothing short of an adventure.

Good photographs of grizzlies rarely come easy. Even with today's excellent telephoto lenses (the 400mm–600mm are the most commonly used), to take an acceptable, publishable photo of a grizzly requires that the photographer get somewhere within seventy to a maximum of two hundred feet of the animal. This range is obviously dangerous, as most grizzlies will not usually tolerate man that close. Even bears that are fairly even-tempered (relatively speaking) show signs of unease at this distance.

On my first trip to Denali National Park, Alaska, I made a mistake that, for several minutes, seemed as though it might cost me my life. That year I had to depend on the shuttle buses for transportation. I caught a shuttle early one morning out of Denali Park Headquarters in the hope that I might find a grizzly near the road. As the bus crossed Sable Pass, I spotted a female and two fully grown cubs feeding one hundred feet off the road. Shuttle-bus drivers (at the direction of the National Park Service) refuse to drop passengers off near a grizzly. A quarter mile later, I managed to convince the driver to let me out.

"You're crazy," the driver grumbled as I stepped from the vehicle.

"Maybe so," I said, "but I'm going to walk back to those bears."

The Alaskan tundra was eerily silent as the sound of the bus faded in the distance. Bushy willows grew ten feet tall on either side of the road, and a dwarf birch occasionally popped up above the thick, knee-high brush that covered the hillside. There were no trees in sight. With my cameras still in their bag and my tripod over my shoulder, I set off, back toward the bears.

A hundred yards later, I rounded a bend and came face to face with one of the cubs. He was a cub in name only. A grizzly female normally breeds only every third or fourth year, and her young may stay with her until she breeds again. This bear, a two and one-half year old, stood staring at me; he was twenty feet away, almost fully grown, and weighed close to three hundred pounds.

Grizzly country, Denali National Park, Alaska

I couldn't see the female or the other cub, but it seemed logical that they, too, might be traveling in my direction. I had never been this close to a grizzly before, and my enthusiasm for photographing them suddenly began to wane. By now, the security of the bus seemed tremendously inviting.

Deciding that the prudent thing to do would be to surrender the road to the bear, I moved about fifteen feet off the gravel surface and watched anxiously as the bear slowly continued up the road. He eyed me as he passed by. He stopped again about fifty feet away, turned around, stared at me a few seconds, and then started walking back in my direction. I decided it was time to start retreating. As I slowly made my way through the brush, the young grizzly followed; it was as though I had piqued his curiosity. I took two steps, and so did he. When I stopped, he stopped. It was a game of cat and mouse, and I was the mouse. For about one hundred fifty yards, the grizzly followed me through the brush, sometimes trailing barely twenty feet behind.

As I moved parallel to the road, uncertain as to where I was headed, I saw the other cub—he also spotted me. The second cub took note of the fun his brother was having and came through the brush toward us. Soon, the two grizzlies had joined ranks and continued to follow me at whatever pace I set. A moment later, I looked ahead and saw the female still feeding near the road. I had done an excellent job placing myself squarely between a she-grizzly and her cubs. A newspaper headline—"Grizzlies Slay Photographer"—passed through my mind.

This thought disappeared when I heard the welcome sound of an engine. A second tour bus was pulling to a stop about one hundred yards away. I could see tourists at the bus windows snapping pictures of me and the bears. "You may have a real show here in a minute," I thought.

Slowly, I edged toward the bus. The cubs matched each of my steps, clinging like shadows. When I had moved to within one hundred feet of the bus, I couldn't stand the tension any longer. With the cubs about forty feet behind me, I dropped my camera bag and tripod and took off at a dead run for the bus. Over my shoulder, I saw the cubs put on a burst of speed.

Within a few seconds, I neared the bus and saw the driver swing the door open wide. My heart was pounding and I thundered into the vehicle, much to the delight of the tourists. Looking back out the window, I saw the cubs inspecting my camera bag. As they sniffed it, I was thankful I hadn't put any food in it that morning. Dropping the bag where I did probably saved me from a rough working-over. The female grizzly ignored the whole incident.

After that episode, I vowed to never again lose control of a photographing session with grizzlies, or to get between a female and her cubs. I would be constantly on the alert for signs that a grizzly may be distressed by my presence. I would always observe a

Grizzly cubs frequently engage in wrestling matches; this not only entertains them but also builds strength and endurance.

bear at a distance to determine its mood and personality before approaching within camera range. However, the best-laid plans of men and photographers do not seem applicable to the grizzly.

It was the second year in Denali National Park that I met Dale Johnson, a cinematographer from South Dakota who was trying to get 16mm movie footage of grizzlies for a film on Alaska. One September morning, Dale and I were driving on the road that parallels Igloo Creek when we spotted a blonde grizzly feeding on soapberries a few hundred yards in the distance. This was a bear that we had seen previously, and after conferring, we decided that we might be safely able to photograph at close range. We mounted our cameras on tripods and moved to a small knoll a short distance off the road and watched the blonde bear feed and slowly move in our direction.

The grizzly was in a thick array of willows, dwarf birch, and smaller brush. The autumn foliage around her was subtlely shaded with hues of red, yellow, and orange. The morning mist cast a gentle gloom across the landscape, and fog drifted in and out again. Tension hung in the air as the bear moved closer through the mist.

After several minutes the bear had closed within a good camera range of less than one hundred feet. Dale and I were a little nervous. The nearest tree was perhaps three miles away. If she charged, running was out of the question.

As the female fed, she continued to move closer to us. Now and then, her massive head came up and out of the brush; she seemed to peer at us with a steely, penetrating gaze. We watched for any indication that she may be unhappy with our presence in her territory, but there was none. The hair on her neck was not raised in alarm, and she made no noise other than the grunting sounds common to the gathering of a berry breakfast.

At seventy feet, she swung her head up again to inspect us, and then, without warning, charged! Branches snapped like twigs as she rushed toward us. We could see her open jaws and hear her heavy breathing. The hair on *my* neck stood erect, and the muscles in my back tightened. There was nowhere to run. Dale and I both knew that we must stand our ground.

When the grizzly closed to within fifty feet, Dale and I began waving our arms furiously and shouting, but the bear kept coming. When she was forty feet away, I mentally prepared myself to hit the ground and curl up in a fetal position.

At thirty feet, the grizzly stopped her charge. She hissed and swung her head from side to side; ominous snarls came from her mouth. For a few terrifying seconds, we stood eye to eye with the most powerful creature on the continent.

Then, with slow, deliberate motions, Dale and I picked up our tripods and began to back away from the angry bear. When we had moved fifteen feet, she resumed feeding, giving us clearance to get back to the car. My hands were shaking so badly I could hardly remove the camera from the tripod.

That same year in Alaska, I observed a particular female and cub several times. Each time I saw her, she was on the move, rolling like a furry locomotive over one hill or another. She appeared to have something less than a stable personality, so I made a mental note to stay clear of this bear. It was a promise that I would not be able to keep.

Late one afternoon on the first day of September, I was perched on a grassy knoll peering through my 400mm lens at a red fox pup about twenty feet away. I had spent the last forty five minutes carefully approaching him across the autumn tundra, purposely ignoring him, as if fox pictures were the last thing I had in mind. This type of psychology usually works when photographing wildlife, and it was working well on this fox.

The young fox was the last member of his family to remain near the den, which was located on a grassy slope about two hundred feet above a gravel bar. His parents and three litter mates had gone their separate ways, dissolving family ties. On my initial approach, I had taken off my backpack—which contained the rest of my camera gear and lunch—and left it on a gravel bar. I then proceeded in the direction of the fox with a tripod-mounted camera and 400mm lens.

The little guy was amazingly tolerant. As I was

This grizzly first charged, then turned and retreated; his irritation is clear both in his look and in the erect hair on his neck.

making my slow approach, he ignored me; he would lie down alongside his den, then get up, stretch and yawn, totally unconcerned by my presence. When I reached the grassy knoll just twenty feet away from him, he merely watched me curiously. I was thrilled at the prospect of shooting a few rolls of film with the red fox at such close range.

As soon as I began clicking off some nice portrait shots of the fox, I suddenly heard a loud "awhoof! awhoof!", combined with the sound of breaking brush. I looked up to see the familiar female grizzly, trailed close behind by her spring cub, tearing furiously down the slope about one hundred fifty feet away. If the bears saw me, they gave no indication, for they ran right by, crossed the gravel bar within fifty feet of my backpack, and continued swiftly across the flat tundra toward the park road a quarter mile away. I breathed a sigh of relief as I watched the two bears move away, grateful that I didn't tangle with this particular grizzly.

My joy was short-lived. As the bears neared the road, a pickup truck bouncing down the gravel highway suddenly increased its speed and cut directly in front of the approaching bears, causing them to turn one hundred eighty degrees and head straight back in my direction.

The little fox stood perfectly still, nervous and tense (feelings I shared), watching the bears close the

---

A sow grizzly rests, but her cub is more curious.

distance between us. When the female grizzly had almost reached my pack on the gravel bar, I shouted loudly, bringing her and the trailing cub to a screeching halt. With this sudden noise, the already-nervous fox came unglued and scrambled back into its den. Meanwhile, the massive female bear whoofed and hissed, pacing back and forth in an angry frenzy, unsure of what to do next. Combined with the bawling of the cub behind her the sound was enough to unravel the most steadfast of nerves. After a moment, much to my joy, the female collected her exhausted cub, and together they galloped up the gravel bar, disappearing from view.

Only one time have I ever had a situation in which I felt that I was in complete control while photographing grizzlies. I still wonder how I could have been so naive.

The following summer, in Canada's Jasper National Park, I spotted two sibling grizzlies cavorting about on a wooded hillside. I watched these two bears and tried to figure out how best to approach them. Then I noticed a deep chasm bisecting the hillside. The bears began to feed near the edge of this gorge, and I concluded that I would be perfectly safe photographing them from the opposite side.

I sneaked into the spruce forest and set up my tripod and camera directly across the gap from the busy bruins. Never had I felt more secure photographing the grizzly at close range. The bears started moving up their side of the chasm, nervously aware

Having misplaced his mother in a field of summer flowers, this cub stands for a better view. In summer, grizzlies find high mountain meadows good grazing grounds, rich in succulent plants, bulbs, and tubers.

of my presence, but unafraid. I was a little frustrated in trying to get pictures, as the light was marginal and required a slow shutter speed with my 400mm lens. In addition, the bears didn't stop long enough for me to get in good position to shoot through the heavy growth of trees.

When one of the bears ambled off up the hill into the brush near the chasm, I thought little of it. Soon, however, the second bear followed his brother into the brush and out of sight. I continued slowly along side the rocky gorge, trying to see what they were up to. One quiet step at a time, I moved in the direction the grizzlies had gone. When I came up over a small knoll and peered around a spruce tree, I felt the adrenaline start to flow—the thirty-foot-wide chasm had dwindled to a mere six feet. Here the two grizzlies had easily made the jump across. We were now all on the same side, and the bears were deliberately making their way, at a fast walk, toward one very frightened photographer.

The grizzlies closed to sixty feet in the heavy timber. Not enthusiastic about having them come any closer, I waved my arms rapidly and shouted. Fortunately, that seemed to be sufficient. Their heads came up, they sniffed the air, and then bolted, running back into the woods. I headed back to my truck. So much for "Plan B."

On another occasion in Alaska, I spotted two grizzlies playing in a pond about half a mile below me. A long, sloping ridge led to the water, and I decided to take this route to the bears. The crest of the ridge was open, but both sides were overgrown with thick willows, the kind of terrain I usually avoid in grizzly country.

The air was calm as I moved down the ridge; my route hugged the line of the willows, and I hoped the bears wouldn't see me or pick up my scent. The female grizzly and her two-year-old cub wrestled playfully in the middle of the pond, and I knew their antics would provide some great pictures. Another minute or so I'll be in good camera range, I thought.

My attempt failed. When I was two hundred yards from the bears, they peered in my direction, rose on their hind legs for a better look, and sniffed. Splashing across the pond, they then bolted into the brush. When they appeared farther up the hillside, I was surprised to see not two bears, but three. The third grizzly, I assumed, must have been hidden near the pond.

Later, I ran into two hikers who had witnessed the entire incident from a nearby ridge.

"Are you the one who was sneaking up on those grizzlies down by the pond?" they wanted to know.

"Yeah, but I didn't get very close," I replied.

"You got a lot closer than you think," said one of the hikers. "The whole time you were walking near the tangle of willows, that third grizzly was stalking you. He probably was within a hundred feet before he turned and headed back to the pond."

Evidently, the second grizzly cub had wandered away from the pond and had either seen or scented me. He may have approached me just out of curiosity, but the thought that a bear could actually get so close to me without my knowledge gave me an incredible feeling of powerlessness.

You don't always have to look for grizzlies in order to find them. Photographing grizzlies that have on numerous occasions wandered through my campsites saves me the trouble of going out to look for them. However, most of my opportunities have been spoiled by bad weather, bad light, or just plain bad luck, resulting in very few good photographs.

While camping in a pup tent in Alaska's Denali National Park, I woke one morning with the sensation that I wasn't alone. Lying motionless for a few seconds, hearing nothing, I decided it was time to get up and get moving. Sitting inside my tent, I was greeted by a loud snort from directly outside. This was followed by a series of "awhoofs" that rapidly drifted away from me toward Igloo Creek, a couple of hundred feet away. I dressed quickly, grabbed my camera, and slid out of my tent. Moving quietly down to the creek, I saw the grizzly just as he disappeared into a thick patch of willows a hundred yards downstream. Not caring to follow him into that thick jungle, I retreated to the tent, where I noticed a huge pile of bear scat squarely on top of one of the tent pegs. I wondered how long the bear had been investigating my camp before I woke up.

The thought of that grizzly outside my tent was

unnerving, but I realized that if I was going to camp in grizzly country, it was conceivable that the bears were going to make nightly patrols of my campsite, and I might just as well accept it, or stay out of the area altogether.

It was not uncommon to have grizzlies pass through my camp along Igloo Creek that fall in Denali. All food was placed in a pack and strung between two trees twelve feet above the ground, and as a result, the bears were never troublesome. They would amble through the campsite and head for the creek, where they would feed on a bumper crop of soapberries.

That particular fall, a female grizzly with three spring cubs made Igloo Creek a prime feeding area. About every three to four days, I would see them raking in berries. I had terrible luck trying to photograph them. It was either too dark, raining, or the bears were in heavy brush whenever I saw them.

Late one afternoon, I returned to camp famished and exhausted. It was misting slightly, so I put my camera gear inside the tent. As I began to lower my food pack to see which kind of noodles I would have for supper, I was startled by a loud bawling from about sixty feet away. Following the direction of the noise, I saw a grizzly cub standing in the bushes. Soon, another and then one more appeared, forming a semi-circle around my tent. I quickly raised my food pack up between the trees and started looking for a tree myself. Immediately, mother bear ap-

peared, and I breathed a sigh of relief as I watched her collect her cubs and move out of my campsite, over to the creek, where they began eating soapberries. Here, finally, I was able to photograph the female and her cubs feeding peacefully on their chosen fare.

Most of my camp photography has largely been nonproductive, but the experiences of bear contact have been enriching, though a little tension-filled. It was to the credit of the bear that he has neither been troublesome nor made any effort to get into the food supply. (The same cannot be said of the ground squirrel, who will take every opportunity given to chew up any food pack left unguarded on the ground for even a few seconds.)

Not all confrontations between grizzly and photographer are serious—sometimes, they take on comic tones. Last fall, another photographer and I were traveling along the Denali National Park road in Alaska searching for grizzlies.

As we drove over Sable Pass, we saw three vehicles—all belonging to wildlife photographers—parked alongside the road. Opposite the vehicles stood three grizzles, a female with her two two and one-half-year-old cubs, feeding about one hundred yards away from the road. We parked behind the last vehicle, got out, and started shooting. The female and one cub gradually moved away from us, but the third kept coming closer. Photographers live for close shots in good light, so everyone continued to expose film at a furious rate.

A good photographer, however, knows when a subject is too close. As the grizzly came within twenty feet of the road, all of us dove simultaneously for the safety of our vehicles. As my colleague and I tried to jam our extended tripods into the front seat, the six tripod legs became entangled, and neither of us could close his door.

Meanwhile, a third photographer had abandoned all hope of returning to his vehicle and was trying desperately to get into my back seat.

"Unlock the !*&★•? door, Carey!" he yelled at me as the bear came nearer. I finally managed to flip the electric door lock, and he scrambled in. While the grizzly thoroughly chewed a film pack left on the ground in front of the car, the tripods were accommodated, and all doors were secured.

Periodically, the grizzly raised its head above the hood and contemplated the three worried faces staring back at him. We speculated on the odds of the three hundred pound bear coming at us through the windshield.

Dale Johnson's jeep stood in front of us. One of the photographers, in a frantic hurry to get away from the bear, had scrambled on to the luggage rack atop the jeep. The grizzly, finally noticing this high-perched photographer, stood on its hind legs and reached for the man. Like a nervous boxer in the ring with a champion, the man managed to dodge the grizzly's half-hearted swipes. Eventually, a symphony of car horns discouraged the bruin, and he wandered off.

About that time, the other two bears decided to get in on the fun. One of the vehicles was a pickup truck with a camper, the kind with a standard door in the rear. It was at the rear of this truck that the bears congregated. Their interest in the back of the pickup continued, and it suddenly dawned on the vehicle's owner that the camper door was open.

Within minutes, the bears confirmed his hunch. Around the side of the pickup they came, each snout covered with the white powder of what was to be the next day's sourdough pancakes.

The photo session was definitely over. Even though the bears hung around for some time, striking all sorts of appropriate poses, there is little market for photos of grizzlies with pancake flour covering their faces.

Profile
of a Grizzly

In a remote winter den in January, grizzlies enter the world with eyes closed, and fine, barely visible hairs on a body that weighs about a pound. These helpless little creatures (who weigh less than a newborn porcupine) huddle close to their mother for warmth and also to receive the nutritious rich milk that will promote a remarkable growth rate. This milk comes from a female bear that hasn't eaten since she denned up in late October or November and won't eat again until she emerges from the den in April or May.

The cubs (twins being common—triplets, quadruplets, or a lone cub the exception) grow at a rapid

Cubs are constantly in search of playthings.

rate and may weigh ten pounds or more when they break out of the security of their den in the spring.

When the cubs enter this bright new world, they can hardly contain themselves. They are furry balls of perpetual motion, and their never-ending curiosity (a trait possessed by all grizzlies) frequently leads them to new discoveries. The cubs stick their inquisitive noses into every nook and cranny. Sticks, rocks, leaves and bones are indiscriminately picked up and examined, chewed and forgotten, as new playthings are found.

The cubs love to engage in spirited wrestling matches that quite frequently are followed by tearing chases, which in turn end in a tangled heap of fur and paws.

Autumn cubs

At seven months, these cubs resemble toys far more than fierce predators.

The cubs are conscientious imitators of their mother. If she digs, they will dig; if she flips over a rock, they also will do the same; when she stands up in alarm, the cubs follow suit.

Females occasionally take time out to romp with their offspring, especially if there is a single cub. In this case, she assumes a dual role: a mother and a companion. The bond between a female and a lone cub seems to be much greater than that of a female with two or more cubs. Twins rely on each other for companionship, but a lone cub must rely on its mother.

All of this activity requires a great deal of energy, which makes the fast-growing cubs forever hungry. The female accommodates them by laying on her back while her little ones crawl on her belly and nurse. She will caress them as they feed, occasionally jerking herself upright if one gets overanxious and bites down too hard. She nurses them regularly at various points during the day, each session lasting three or four minutes. These feeding sessions are quite often followed by naps.

The female grizzly is very protective of her cubs and won't hesitate to fight if she thinks they are being threatened. One August morning on Sable Pass in Denali National Park, I was watching a female with her two half-grown cubs feeding about a quarter of a mile away. Around me, the heavy mist that shrouded the surrounding peaks was lifting and the sun began breaking through the clouds, promising a brighter day after three miserable ones of solid rain. I had been watching the bears for about a half hour when a distant movement caught my eye. Coming down a high misty slope was another female with her three small spring cubs. This female, with the little ones trailing close behind, was heading straight for the grazing bears below, each family unaware of the other's presence.

As the gap between them narrowed to a hundred yards, the approaching female stopped and stood up, imitated by her three small cubs. About the same time, the other female with the older offspring sensed the approach and without hesitation, charged. The first female sent the three little cubs scurrying back up the slope and then she, too, charged, meeting the oncoming rush. In a terrible rage, they both stood, biting and pawing each other and emitting full-throated roars that easily carried down to me. Meanwhile, the three small cubs were bawling frantically, frenziedly standing and sitting as the fight continued. The older cubs paced nervously back and forth, but remained more in control. The two females battled for about a half a minute and then settled down to a face-off on all fours, growling and snorting. Then they separated and returned to their respective famiilies.

Shortly after, the female, with the three spring cubs crowding her closely, came down to within fifty yards of the other bears. All seven fed peacefully, and fifteen minutes later, went their separate ways. The females had not hesitated to defend their cubs. But what was most interesting was that mutual agreement had been reached in a very dramatic fashion between the two she-bears.

Grizzly cubs occasionally fall victim to other bears, despite the mother's fearless protective instinct.

Frederick Dean, professor of Wildlife Management, University of Alaska, Fairbanks, told me about a very unusual observation that he made in May of 1984 in Denali National Park. (The full account is scheduled to appear in an upcoming issue of the Canadian *Field-Naturalist*.)

Dean and two companions had stopped their vehicle about a mile from the Toklat river to watch a female grizzly with two yearling cubs digging for roots among scattered willows, not too far from the road. After watching the bears for about twenty minutes, they noticed a large, light-brown male bear

A female grizzly and her two six-month-old cubs. The sow's rich milk enables the cubs to put on weight rapidly.

Female grizzlies engage in a combative ballet in defense of cubs and feeding grounds.

emerge from the willows and at a fast walk, proceed straight for the bear family. When he was about sixty feet away, the big male charged; the female and her yearlings bolted in different directions. The male followed one of the yearlings and when the female saw this, she turned and chased the big male. The male caught the yearling and knocked it over with one swipe of its paw just as the protective female rushed in to attack. The male and female fought savagely, alternately standing on hind legs and then dropping to all fours, biting at each other's heads, necks, and shoulders. Meanwhile, the yearling that had been swiped appeared to be partially paralyzed, as it dragged its hind legs as it escaped to a nearby gravel bar. The other uninjured yearling was not seen again by Dean that day after the initial attack. After fighting for fifteen to twenty minutes, the male bear killed the female. He fed for a few minutes on the carcass and then scraped sand and gravel on it before laying down on top of it.

The injured yearling dragged itself to a point about three hundred yards from the carcass and was ignored by the large male. This yearling was shot by park rangers five days later, as it had virtually no chance to survive. The large male stayed near the dead female for about two days and then wasn't seen near it again. He had fed very little on the carcass.

Over the next few weeks, the uninjured yearling was seen periodically near its dead mother. Three weeks after the incident, Dean saw this same year-ling within twenty-five yards of the carcass. Upon inspecting the female's body, Dean thought that it appeared that something had been recently sucking one of its nipples.

The preceding accounts demonstrate how determined a female grizzly is when it comes to defending her young. But what will she do with it if it is killed? There are many accounts of grizzlies killing and feeding on the carcass of other bears. Will a female feed on her dead offspring?

Gary Gregory, the Resource Manager in Glacier National Park, Montana, told me about a case of cannibalism that he witnessed in the fall of 1984. In a horse pasture at Quarter-Circle bridge near the park headquarters, Gary observed a female grizzly with her single yearling cub feeding on a dead horse for a couple of days. Several days later, Gary witnessed this same female feeding on her dead cub. It wasn't clear how the cub died; it is very unlikely the female would have killed her own cub. At this time, there were other bears in the area and it was assumed that one of these had killed the cub during a conflict over the dead horse. At any rate, once the cub was killed, the female lost her protective instinct and commenced to feed on the carcass.

The majority of the grizzly's time is spent feeding or in search of food. Grizzlies must eat copiously and continuously in order to build a supply of fat that can carry them through the winter denning period.

A wet mountain grizzly feeds on soapberries in Denali National Park.

They are carnivorous by evolution, but omnivorous by necessity; they must rely on vegetation for about ninety percent of their diet. Their molars have evolved to crush and grind their vegetable diet. Grasses, nuts, seeds, roots, bulbs, twigs are some of the things on the grizzly's menu. A variety of berries—blueberries and buffalo berries—are eaten in season. I have watched grizzlies feeding hour after hour on soapberries in Alaska in the fall. During this time, they leave huge scat piles full of undigested berries scattered throughout their feeding area. Evidently, though, they digest enough of them to make it worth the effort.

Most people's conception of the grizzly is that of a predator: stalking elk, moose, or caribou and then closing in for the kill. It is true that these bears will eat meat in about any stage of decay, because they are not all that adept at killing it themselves. One big exception are ground squirrels; I've watched many grizzlies spend countless hours in pursuit of this meager fare with a fair amount of success. But, contrary to popular belief, the typical grizzly doesn't often have that kind of luck with bigger game. It is unlikely that a grizzly will even attempt to tackle a healthy, large mammal, simply because the bear hasn't the speed to catch it. It may also be that grizzlies recognize that large mammals can kick or gore them. There have been several observations made in Alaska of cow moose driving grizzlies away from their calves. Also, I believe that there are grizzlies who don't know how to kill big game. I have watched grizzlies walk by elk in Yellowstone National Park and caribou in Alaska, barely giving them a second look. That is not to say, however, that a grizzly won't take advantage of a situation when the opportunity presents itself.

When big game animals such as elk, moose, and caribou are calving, the newborn are especially vulnerable to predators during their first week or two. Wolves, coyotes, cougars, and sometimes grizzlies take a certain percentage of these young. Some grizzlies in Yellowstone National Park head for the calving grounds of elk in the spring and have been observed chasing and killing elk calves.

In some areas in the Yukon and Alaska, game biologists have evidence of grizzlies killing large numbers of newborn moose. Occasionally, grizzlies kill adult big game, but in most cases, only when these animals are in a weakened condition from a hard winter, sick, or injured.

In Denali National Park several years ago Gordon Haber, a biologist doing research on predators, observed grizzlies and wolves moving into areas where moose were rutting. A number of times, Haber found evidence of grizzlies and wolves making double kills on bull moose who had fought to the point of exhaustion.

In the spring, grizzlies search along avalanche chutes with the prospect of finding mountain goat or bighorn sheep carcasses, animals killed by being

When they can be found, insects are a favorite part of the grizzly's menu.

swept from their mountain perch. The grizzly also treks across big game ranges looking for winter kills or animals too weak to outrun him. When he does find a carcass, he will feed on it with relish, no matter how rotten the meat. Once he lays claim to it, he may move it to another location, cover it with leaves, grass, or dirt, and defend it with utter ferocity.

Asa Brooks told me about an observation he had made in early August several years ago while working as a naturalist in Glacier National Park. A packer hauling supplies to a trail crew lost a mule that had slipped and plunged over a cliff about five miles north of Granite Park Chalet on the Highline trail. A few days after, Brooks who led nature walks from Logan Pass, took a dozen tourists up the Highline trail to see if anything interesting was feeding on the mule carcass. After the long hike, the hikers quietly rounded a bend on the trail about two hundred yards above the dead mule and were surprised to see two grizzlies and two wolverines around the carcass.

The larger of the two grizzlies was feeding on the mule, while the smaller bear waited cautiously back a few yards. One of the wolverines was also feeding on the carcass and the other was back about twenty yards or so. The small group of people hadn't been there long when the feeding wolverine, engrossed in its meal, moved too close to the large grizzly. The big bear, angry at the intrusion, turned its head and with its left forepaw backhanded the wolverine, striking the smaller animal in the head.

The wolverine rolled backward and collapsed in a lifeless heap, its neck broken. The other wolverine, not wanting any part of the big bear, did an about-face and loped off into the timber and was not seen again. Meanwhile, the larger grizzly continued its feeding while the smaller bear walked around behind him, picked up the dead wolverine in its jaws, and carried it about twenty yards to a large, car-sized boulder. This grizzly then proceeded to climb up on the rock and, with the wolverine still in his jaws, stood up on his hind legs and shook the devil out of it. Whether this grizzly was venting its frustration at not being able to feed on the dead mule goes unanswered, but he did, at any rate, put on quite a show. The grizzlies fed on the carcasses for a while longer and then retreated to a large snowfield, where they laid down to cool off.

The grizzly's strength and endurance are legendary. Grizzlies can move huge boulders with a minimum of effort just to get at a ground squirrel, and it is said that a single swipe of one of the bear's forepaws can break a domestic bull's neck. It takes a lot of strength to drag the carcass of a thousand-pound bull elk or an even larger bull moose up the slope of a mountain, but a grizzly has that capacity.

A NPS maintenance operator was driving along the Firehole River on a spring day a number of years ago when he saw a grizzly dragging a bull-elk carcass across the river. The operator stopped his truck and watched as the bear reached the opposite side

*Observing the approach
of another bear*

33

and pushed the carcass up on the river bank. The grizzly had to let go of the body to climb up on the bank, and the elk carcass slid back into the water. The grizzly repeated the maneuver with the same result. After the elk slid back into the water the second time, the grizzly became furious. Much to the man's surprise, the grizzly got under the carcass and with his powerful forepaws, threw it up over the six-foot bank on to level ground and then easily dragged it off into the timber.

During the course of the year, grizzlies may range over areas as small as twenty square miles or as large as several hundred square miles. Bears have home ranges but don't defend them from other bears. In fact, there is considerable home-range overlap. Thus, bears cannot be strictly described as "territorial" animals.

Grizzlies normally don't live in groups although they do congregate at highly productive feeding areas such as spawning salmon streams, or lush berry patches, or, unfortunately, garbage dumps. And of course, there are females with cubs and grizzly couples during the mating season that spend time together. Otherwise, grizzlies normally give each other wide berths.

When there are congregations of grizzlies at feeding areas, the dominant bears, usually the larger males, get the choicest locations. Depending on the individual bear, each will have a certain restricted space of varying size, within which they will not tolerate another bear. This space can include an entire berry patch.

One rainy August afternoon, a photographer friend, Jess Lee, and I were watching a small, beautiful honey-colored grizzly feeding on soapberries along the Toklat River in Denali National Park. We had been watching this bear feeding for about a half an hour when suddenly he began to behave in a very nervous manner. He kept looking to our left, alternately standing with nose lifted to pick up a scent and then dropping to all fours. He did this for almost a minute before he suddenly turned away from whatever he had sensed, and bolted. The little grizzly made a quick exit out of the berry patch, tearing within one hundred fifty feet of Jess and me, not even giving us a glance. He bounded up a high, steep, sandy bluff behind us and stopped at the top, turned, and nervously looked back to the soapberry patch.

Jess and I were also curious as to what had caused the flight of the little bear. We both knew that the only thing that would probably chase a grizzly out of a berry patch would be a bigger grizzly. Our guess was proven when a large, dark-brown bear appeared from a stand of willows and commenced to feed on soapberries two hundred yards away, too far to photograph. We turned our attention back to the little grizzly who had since lain down facing us, with his nose cradled between his front paws; he looked curiously like a friend's yellow labrador. The little grizzly appeared to have lost his best friend. He stayed down for a couple of minutes, sat up on his haunches, and then lay back down again, always with his eyes trained on the bigger grizzly. After about ten minutes on the sandy bluff, the little grizzly must have gathered up some courage or was experiencing extreme hunger pains, as he began to angle down the bluff in the direction of the berry patch. He again passed within throwing distance, paying us no heed. The small bear had just reached the edge of the soapberry patch when suddenly, the dark brown grizzly, furious at the intrusion, charged. Even though the big grizzly stopped his charge at the patch's perimeter, the smaller bear beat a retreat and continued back down the river bed at a pace that didn't slow even after he was far distant.

In late October or November, with arctic air and flurries of snow signaling the onslaught of winter, grizzlies retreat to their winter quarters. It is believed that the lack of food, combined with winter snows, are what usually drive the bears into their dens. If the bear is healthy, he will have adequate fat reserves to carry him through the winter. Spring cubs, usually yearlings and occasionally some two-year-olds, will den with their mother. The dens are normally located on north-facing slopes at high elevations; deep layers of snow insulate the bears from winter's wrath.

Dens might be dug under the spreading roots of large trees, stumps, boulders, or straight into a mountain slope—anything that will provide solid support. Dry grass, pine boughs, or other vegetation are quite often used to cover the den floor. Grizzlies may use old dens but are more likely to dig new ones each year.

Once they enter their den in the fall to hibernate, grizzlies generally don't eat or drink until they emerge in the spring. Their body temperature drops a few degrees and their heart beat slows considerably, and as a result, they use less oxygen. Unlike other hibernators, such as marmots and ground squirrels who go into a deep, almost unconscious state, grizzlies sleep less soundly and are easily awakened. Grizzlies have been reported moving about during mid-winter, but this is usually the result of disturbance, extremely mild weather, or extreme hunger.

Yearling grizzly cubs normally spend the second summer with their mother and in some areas, den with her the following winter. If the cubs are still with the female in their third spring, she will drive them off when she's ready to mate. In the case where there are two or more offspring, this probably isn't all that traumatic for the cubs, as the bond between them is probably tighter than that with their mother. Quite often, these siblings will remain together the rest of the summer and they may even den together. Eventually, this pairing loosens and they go their separate ways.

In the case of a single cub, where the bond be-

With her cubs paying close attention, a sow grizzly digs furiously for ground squirrel.

tween female and cub is closer, more force may be required by the mother bear to run her cub off. Without a companion, this cub undoubtedly would feel rather forlorn for awhile.

Sometimes, grizzly cubs will remain with the female through the third summer, but only if she doesn't breed in the spring. I have seen a number of females, each with two and one-half-year-old cubs, in Denali in August and September over a four-year period. Although the cubs wandered considerably, they did more-or-less remain together as a loose family unit. On two occasions, I have seen these two and one-half-year-olds nursing. Whether these cubs were allowed to den with the female or wandered off and denned separately I don't know. Regardless, the female would have probably mated the following spring and neither she nor the male would have tolerated the cubs' presence.

Grizzly females usually breed every three or four years and in a few instances, every other year. Females normally don't reach sexual maturity until they are at least four-and-one-half-years old. The mating season for grizzlies runs primarily from the end of May, peaking in June, sometimes stretching into the first part of July. When females come into heat, males move in, anxious to accommodate them. The mating season is normally the only time that adult grizzly males and females tolerate one another.

Sow grizzly and twins

Quite often, a male and female will pair up and stay together as long as the female is in heat. During this courtship time, they will nuzzle each other and play affectionately. The grizzlies might mate three or four times or more per day. If another male tries to move in, the dominant of the two will drive the other off, or, if they are fairly equally matched, a furious fight may develop. In either case, the males seldom tolerate another male near the female. But, as in most aspects of bear behavior, there are exceptions.

An example of this is an observation in 1941 made by Adolph Murie and published in his book, *A Naturalist in Alaska*. Over a period of about three weeks in what is now Denali National Park, Murie observed two males and a female grizzly together during the spring mating season. During this time, he observed the three grizzlies sleeping side by side on different occasions. Both males were seen mating with the female over a three-week period. Although it is quite common for males to mate with different females over the course of the breeding season, it is unusual for two males to tolerate each other's presence in the company of a female in estrus.

By the first or second week of July, the grizzly mating season has essentially ended. At this time, the bears usually return to their solitary lives. The males will not assume any parental responsibility the following spring and, in fact, will not be tolerated anywhere near the cubs. A true grizzly family does not make room for father.

The Lighter Side
of the Grizzly

It was a beautiful afternoon, uncommonly warm for early September in Denali National Park, with only a few puffs of clouds drifting lazily over the vast tundra.

The bear I was observing fed with utter gluttony on the bonanza of berries. After gorging himself, he decided it was time for a nap in the warm autumn sun, and lay down on his belly, nose between paws. About this time, a second grizzly appeared over the crest of a high and barren ridge about a quarter-mile away. As he ambled down along the flank of this

This grizzly interrupted his rambles to sit down and scratch; a few seconds later, he resumed his trek through the sleet storm.

ridge, he suddenly stopped, alert and tense, his head swinging slowly back and forth, his nose pointed slightly upward, testing the breeze. He froze, his eyes trained on the reclining grizzly below him. He began to walk in the direction of the other bear, slowly at first; he suddenly broke into a loping run as he made his way down the slope. When the bear reached the flat, he slowed but continued at a fast pace until he was about seventy-five yards from the napping grizzly. Tentative now, the approaching bear slowly stalked his unwitting adversary until he was about twenty feet from the snoozing grizzly, who was still basking in the sun. If the intent of the approaching bear was to play a practical joke, it

Mountain grizzly

worked marvelously. He let out a short whoof and the sleeping grizzly snapped out of his dreams into a flurry of motion.

Instead of defending his position, the surprised grizzly immediately took off in an all-out run. Ten-foot willows became no obstacle as the prankster closed from behind. Shortly they were lost from view, but I could follow their direction of travel by the waving of willows and the sound of breaking branches. About three hundred yards from where he was surprised, the leading grizzly reached another open ridge and rushed up the slope, the second bear in close pursuit. The pace slackened to a fast walk as the two bears, fat from a long summer of voracious feeding, became winded from climbing the ever-steepening ridge. Finally, they dropped off the top of the crest and out of sight, the pursuant about twenty feet behind. The outcome of the game is known only to the participants.

It is a sad fact that most people are alerted only to grizzly accounts that entail vicious attacks on man. These accounts are invariably carried by all the news media nationwide. Add to this Hollywood's fictionalized horror movies about huge, man-eating grizzlies, and it becomes more apparent why the public sees only the bad side of this powerful animal. There does exist another, less sensational side to these bears that is quite interesting.

One warm and sunny afternoon in May, I was climbing a steep alder-covered mountain on Kodiak Island with hunting companions Dan Sisson and

A gastronomic opportunist, the grizzly enjoys mutton when the occasion presents itself; more often than not, he must content himself with much smaller game.

43

Bob Cassel, making a long stalk for a brown bear. Dan had a brown bear permit and was also writing about his hunt for *Field & Stream,* while Bob was serving as guide. I was on assignment to photograph for the magazine. The three of us stopped for a short break and were scouting the opposite slopes. Bob spotted a large bear in a narrow, snow-covered avalanche chute high above the timberline. We watched the big brownie move across the chute, lose his grip, and glide on his posterior about thirty feet down the snow-packed slide. He regained his footing and ambled over to a mound of snow and lay down on his belly, spread-eagle, apparently cooling off. After about a half-minute, he got up and crossed the fifty-foot avalanche chute, slipping and sliding across the width to the opposite side. Climbing a short distance, he reached up and put his forepaws (in sort of a bear hug) around a huge mound of snow, pulling it down toward himself. A ball of snow had been created and was now rolling down the bank and onto the steep chute, the big bear loping along right behind it. He chased and swatted it with his huge forepaws until it broke up. The bear then climbed back to the same mound of snow, broke off another chunk, and played the same game once more, chasing it down the chute. After this episode, he climbed the bank and ambled off across the large snowfield, evidently in the search of new adventures.

We had watched in amazement at the large Kodiak bear's display of frivolity, and I secretly wondered how his reputation might suffer were it known by all that he engaged in such undignified displays of pleasure.

Scenes like this are counter to popularly accepted ideas about the great bears in North America. Given the grizzly's violent reputation and the fact that he deports himself with a certain dignity, one would not expect this fierce and solemn creature to engage in any activity that didn't serve basic needs. And yet, the grizzly has a perpetual curiosity about the wondrous world around him that sometimes leads him to outbursts of amusing behavior. Grizzly cubs, especially, seem to delight in their fascinating environment, and are constantly in search of interesting things to stick their inquisitive noses into. With boundless energy, cubs are always looking for an excuse to romp and play; quite often, they are joined by their mother.

Jack Lounsbury, district ranger for the canyon area in Yellowstone National Park, related an amusing observation he had made one spring afternoon. It was the end of May, and while patroling near Hayden Lake, he spied a female with two yearling cubs. The bears were digging up roots and ground squirrels in the huge rolling sagebrush-covered valley, about four hundred yards from the park road. When the grizzlies finished digging, they moved over to a steep northfacing, finger-shaped snowdrift

---

Alarmed at her cubs' absence, a female grizzly races through the snow in search of them.

44

*A small Candian stream
provides limitless entertainment
for this grizzly cub.*

about one hundred yards wide and twenty yards from top to bottom, a remnant of the harsh Yellowstone winter.

The cubs immediately raced down the slope, tumbling and rolling as they went. The female, not to be outdone, took a big leap, landed on her posterior, and slid down the steep drift in a shower of spraying snow, out onto the grass where she was met by her two pouncing, frolicking cubs. The three grizzlies then scampered back up the snowdrift and repeated the whole episode.

For the next forty minutes they slid, rolled, and chased each other up and down the slope in a frenzy of aimless fun. The mother bear was as much in the spirit of the whole thing as were her cubs. Sometimes she would push the cubs or the cubs would push her down the slope. With individual variations, they would glissade down the drift on their bellies,

September snow is a stark background for a sow and her cubs.

their rears, feet first and then head first. A flurry of paws and fur at the bottom of the drift was followed by a brief and good-natured wrestling match.

When the grizzlies finally grew tired of their play, the female moved her cubs to a nearby ridge where she lay on her back with a cub on each side and contentedly nursed the ninety-pound twins.

Grizzlies know their home territory well— where to find the best berry patches, the area with the highest population of ground squirrels, and the lushest grasses. One damp August morning in Denali National Park, I saw a grizzly that had evidently just remembered one of these favorite areas, and was determined to get there despite a few distractions.

The big silvertip grizzly moved along the slope of the mountain in long rolling strides, cutting across the grain of ridges and drainages as he went. As he came over one such ridge and dropped down into a shallow draw, a big bull caribou, who had bedded down for a mid-afternoon nap in a tall patch of willows, came crashing out of its resting spot. The caribou stopped a hundred yards down the slope and turned back to watch the grizzly. The great bear hadn't even broken his stride and was still loping along the same course, seemingly oblivious of the terrified caribou. Two hundred yards ahead, a hiker made his way down from the top of the mountain; seeing that he was on a collision course with the bear, he began to wave his arms and run back up the slope as fast as his legs would carry him. The grizzly,

After having been chased out of a soapberry patch by another grizzly, this small, honey-colored bear waits patiently for the dominant bear to leave before he returns to his feast.

aware of the frantic hiker, veered slightly downward, but hardly gave the man a second look as he continued his journey.

His destination in view, the bear angled straight down to a large drainage, where he found the remembered patch of soapberries. Along the fringe, a covey of ptarmigan exploded in a flurry of flashing wings. The birds, like the previous distractions, were ignored as he found a well-stocked bush and began to feast.

At first, he reached up with one paw and grasped a fruit-laden branch, using his teeth to take in berries, leaves, and twigs. After a while, he sat on his haunches and used both paws in feeding. It wasn't long before he got tired of sitting and lay down, plucking the berries off with amazing dexterity. The last method wasn't quite as efficient, but was no doubt more comfortable for the bear. The grizzly spent the rest of the afternoon in the berry patch, obviously contented.

One of the animals who seems to be near the top of the grizzlies' grocery list is the ground squirrel; I have seen them go to great lengths to obtain this relatively meager fare.

Early one August morning, I watched a straw-colored blonde grizzly amble along an open slope, investigating each hole in the ground, trying to pick up the scent of ground squirrel. I watched him sniff out half a dozen holes before he apparently found one with the inviting aroma of squirrel. Immediate-

ly, the grizzly began a flurry of digging remarkably like a dog, kicking dirt out between his hind legs. This bear had developed a definite procedure, knowledge most likely gained from previous experiences. He dug rapidly for a few seconds, stopped and thumped the ground hard with both front paws, reared up to check the neighboring holes for any sign of a squirrel using an alternate escape route, sniffed the hole once more, and resumed his digging. It was probably the third or fourth time that he thumped the ground that a squirrel came barreling out of the hole right under the grizzly, just as he reared up. The bear dove back under his own belly at the fleeing squirrel, his long claws just missing the small prey. The bear spun around and pounced on the unfortunate squirrel when it was just short of its other den. The grizzly quickly dispatched the squirrel, consuming it in a few gulps.

Fortunately for ground squirrels, not all bears are quite as efficient. One time in early September, I watched a bear lope along a side hill, weaving back and forth, when he suddenly stopped. He quickly veered to the right, surprising a ground squirrel a short distance away from its den. The squirrel sprinted toward its hole and dove in, a whisker ahead of the grizzly's front paw, which slammed down on the hard earth just behind him. The bear immediately began to dig, trying to extricate the squirrel. This grizzly had the finesse of a steam shovel, sending a steady barrage of dirt skyward.

The bear was half-buried when the ground squirrel came scurrying out of another hole, about thirty feet away and dashed up the slope unscathed. I continued to watch the bear for awhile—he was still digging, unaware that the squirrel had long since departed. Eventually his enthusiasm waned; the amount of dirt displaced by the bear gradually slowed down. The prospect of a squirrel dinner rapidly diminishing, the bear finally stopped and climbed out of the chamber that was now big enough to contain him. I could sympathize with the creature's frustration as he slowly lumbered off.

If there was ever a ground squirrel that seemed to be up against impossible odds, it would have to be the one I observed one morning on my last visit to Denali National Park. From a high vantage point, I watched a large grizzly ambling down a dried-up river bed, a couple of miles above where it entered the Toklat River. Islandlike patches of willows grew randomly in the center of the river bed. From one of these came the familiar chirp of a ground squirrel alarm. Then about a hundred feet from the squirrel, the bear froze, pointed his nose upward, and tested the air. After a few seconds, he launched himself with a tearing run into the patch of eight-foot-high willows. The squirrel shot out of the other side, circled behind the bear, and stopped under another

A nervous mountain grizzly observes my approach.

thick growth of foliage. Meanwhile, the grizzly bounded through the brush, alternately rearing up to get a better view, then dropping to all fours; he would then lope off and begin the whole procedure again, still in search of his tiny prey. It wasn't long before, in his determined hunt, the bear nearly stepped on the squirrel, who immediately bolted, closely followed by the bear. Back and forth, around the willows they went, the squirrel weaving through the brush while the bear plowed after it. As this wild chase was taking place, a new participant was about to join in.

A golden eagle, perched on the opposite bluff, seemed to decide that it was time for a quick meal. The eagle came winging down just as the grizzly-pursued squirrel entered a small opening in the river bed. The eagle swooped over the bear's head, talons outstretched for the small prey; it missed by just inches. The grizzly struck in frustration at the winged bandit and in doing so, allowed the lightening-fast quarry to reach the willows once again.

The eagle retreated to its perch on the bluff, and the bear again searched for the elusive squirrel. It wasn't long before the bear had the squirrel on the run again, and the sharp eye of the eagle picked up the movement. Immediately, the bird launched off the bluff, powerful wings driving him downward for the attack. This time, the squirrel took refuge in the willows long before the eagle even got close, so the big bird ended its attack by swooping obstinately near the bear's head, provoking him to swat furiously at the intruder. At that momemt, the squirrel tore across the riverbed and disappeared into some thick vegetation. The grizzly continued to search the area for a while longer, finally admitted defeat, and began his journey down to the Toklat, while the eagle caught some thermals and moved on to easier prey. The ground squirrel had Lady Luck working overtime for him that day.

It has not been my intention to show the grizzly as an innocuous creature incapable of violent acts. I have the utmost respect for his tremendous physical capabilities and unpredictable temperament, and I believe that anyone who disregards this and takes too many liberties is flirting with disaster. However, the grizzly very seldom seeks trouble, and I feel he has not been treated fairly on that account. Were he the predacious beast that has been so often portrayed, I seriously doubt that outdoorsmen, myself included, would be around to amble through grizzly country.

Bear Versus Man

When the grizzly does attack man, the consequences are often far-reaching and long-remembered. Powerlessness is a great source of fear and when the scenario is bear versus man, we are reminded of the grizzly's brute power.

It was midnight, and a full moon shone down on Rainbow Point Campground in the Gallatin National Forest, less than ten miles northwest of West Yellowstone, Montana. A camper sitting near his fire saw a large bear walking around the outer limits of the campground. The bear, which he suspected might be a grizzly, ignored him and disappeared into the night.

Two and a half hours later, at 2:30 a.m. on Saturday, June 25th, in the same campground, two Wisconsin men awoke simultaneously as something began shaking their heavy canvas tent, causing the tent poles to rattle. They could hear no sniffing or growling sounds. Suddenly, the tent collapsed and one of the men screamed as a grizzly tore open a large hole in the tent and dragged him out. The other camper exited through the same hole and stood up. By moonlight, he could see the grizzly standing over his screaming companion only ten feet away.

Quickly, the grizzly grabbed his victim by the ankle and dragged him another thirty feet. Furious as

Grizzlies can be distinguished from black bears by their shoulder hump, their more massive head and body, and their longer claws.

well as terrified, the uninjured man picked up a tent pole and charged the grizzly, yelling and throwing the pole, causing the bear to retreat; he didn't approach his injured friend any closer, but spoke to him, asking, "Are you all right?", to which he received the reply, ". . .I'm not doing so good."

At that point, the uninjured camper returned to the collapsed tent to look for the flashlight, car keys, and glasses. Minutes went by as he frantically searched in the dark; then he heard his companion scream again and suddenly stop. At that time, several other campers came with flashlights, and one went to phone the sheriff's office. The sheriff arrived about ten minutes later. Approximately 3:30 a.m., one hour after the initial attack, the body was found several hundred feet from the campsite, partially consumed.

Details of this attack were repeated nationwide by newspapers, radio, and television stations. It took its place with stories of murder, rape, and terrorist bombings, usual items given top billing. Yet, even though we are conditioned to expect the worst, many believe that humans who commit acts of violence are the exceptions, rather than the rule. Somehow, we retain faith in our fellow man. This is not the case with the grizzly. If one grizzly is a man-eater, then logic tells us that all grizzlies are surely potential man-eaters. In reality, the vast majority of bear-versus-man encounters actually end peacefully, with all participants going their separate ways.

One cold, drizzly Alaskan August evening, I was bending down to get a pan of frigid water out of Igloo Creek when I heard someone yelling a short distance up the park road. My campsite was only several hundred feet downstream from the bridge where Igloo Creek intersected the road. The uproar seemed to be coming from the other side of the bridge.

About that time, a tall, lanky man in his mid-thirties came into view, "picking them up and laying them down" as he raced toward the bridge. About thirty feet behind him, I saw a medium-sized blonde grizzly loping steadily along. The bear looked as if he were on an evening romp, in contrast to the man, who was quite terror stricken. When the man reached the bridge, the grizzly ambled off the road to a large patch of soapberries, as though that had been his original intention. Meanwhile, the sprinter barreled into the campground and stopped once he realized he was no longer being "attacked."

Motivated by curiosity, I walked over to the out-of-breath man and asked him what happened. Regaining his composure, he told me his story: he had left the campground a little earlier to take a walk up the road; about a quarter of a mile from the bridge, he came around a bend and met the grizzly walking down the road toward him, only a couple hundred feet away. For one brief instant, bear and man froze, then the man turned around and began a scrambling retreat back toward the campground, the bear hot on his heels.

What interested me at the time was the behavior

Obviously irritated, this grizzly has just completed a charge initiated by my carelessness in letting him get too close to me; when he stopped, I was able to slowly back away.

of the bear. The grizzly could have easily run down the terrified man. Instead, the bear followed a short distance behind, as if he were satisfying his curiosity.

Grizzlies, not unlike human beings, have different personalities, making it difficult to know how they will react in any given situation. In the majority of the experiences I have had, and of those that have been related to me, the grizzly will turn and run away. Sometimes they get uncomfortably close out of curiosity; once they discover the human scent though, they beat a tearing retreat. Occasionally, a person stumbles upon a bad-tempered bear who, for no apparent reason, will attack. My observations of the bear in most situations, however, indicate that this seems to be the exception rather than the rule.

Bear attacks usually can be traced to one of three basic situations: The grizzly is protecting a food source, such as an animal carcass; a female bear is protecting her cub; or a bear is surprised at close range. The odds of a bear attack in any of these situations escalate dramatically. The grizzly might classify the attack as provoked because he is defending what he knows to be his. In a situation such as this, man becomes a threat to the bear.

Clyde Fauley, Resource Management Specialist in Glacier National Park, told me about one nerve-wracking experience he had in July 1976.

A cold crossing at Igloo Creek, Denali National Park, Alaska.

Returning from a hike along Harrison Creek in the park, he encountered a female grizzly flanked by two, two and one-half year old cubs about one hundred fifty feet ahead of him on the trail. The female, a cub on each side, saw him and charged immediately, stopping at one hundred feet. All three bears raised up on their hind legs, growled and sniffed the air, dropped down, and charged again, this time stopping at thirty-five feet. Fauley had experienced quite a few encounters with grizzlies while working in the park, some of them at close range, but nothing compared to this. After the initial charge, he knew that running or climbing a tree was out of the question, so he resorted to talking to the bears in as calm a voice as he could muster. As the grizzlies closed the gap, he told them about the park's Bear Management Plan, because he couldn't think of anything else to say. As he explained the plan to the three bears, he slowly retreated into a small draw off the trail and out of sight of the bears. Fauley then heard what seemed to be another short charge, providing him with another anxious moment. He couldn't see the bears, so he circled around a small knoll, returned to the now-empty trail, and continued his hike back to West Glacier without further incident.

It is to Fauley's credit that no tragedy resulted from this confrontation. It took a level head to avoid panicking in a very dangerous position. Any other reaction on his part could have prompted an attack by the female and possibly a mauling. One can only

The safest view is of a retreating grizzly.

speculate whether talking made the difference, but an attack was averted.

Through hindsight, we are able to look at cases of man-bear encounters and sometimes determine that decisions made by the people involved may not have always been the best. While judgements are more easily made sitting in a rocking chair versus standing thirty feet from an irritated grizzly, nevertheless, there are cases where people have reacted in an unusual manner in a bear encounter and despite this, have come out relatively unscathed. In these instances, some credit must be given to the behavior of the bear.

In late August of 1982, two companions were hiking along a ridge in late afternoon, about one mile from Teklanika Campground in Denali National Park, when they saw a grizzly about thirty feet ahead of them. One of the men dropped his daypack (which contained some food), and both retreated about fifty yards; they watched the bear devour the contents of the pack. When the bear finished, he approached the men at a fast walk. They threw some cookies toward the bear, then backed off a short distance; again, they watched the grizzly eat this second snack. After the bear finished the cookies, he approached the hikers in the same deliberate manner. When the grizzly was within five feet of the two men, the bear stood up, and they decided it was time to hit the ground and assume a fetal position. Several times, the bear circled the two men curled up on the ground, then approached one, sniffed at his hair, and fogged up his glasses. The grizzly then attempted to pull his tucked-in leg away from his body, at which time the man pulled it back again, startling the bear. The grizzly jumped back, growled, then circled the two men again. He sniffed around them a moment or two, then, almost as an afterthought, bit one hiker in the hindquarters and walked away.

The hiker was fortunate in that the most pain he suffered was not from the two minor puncture wounds in his posterior, but rather, from the tetanus shot given him afterward.

One wonders what might have happened in this encounter if these two men had simply stood their ground, shouted or waved their arms, and slowly backed off without dropping the pack. The bear's reaction in this incident may have only been curiosity. It is to the credit of the grizzly that he didn't react violently.

Since the turn of the century, fourteen people have been killed by grizzlies in the continental United States. Considering the number of man-bear encounters that have taken place over this period of time, this fatality figure is surprisingly low.

Looking back to the 1800s, when the western United States was being settled, there are many accounts of grizzly versus man, only a few resulting in human death. In reading these early accounts, including the well-documented ones from the Lewis and Clark expedition, we find that many bear attacks were the result of humans greeting the bears behind the barrel of a rifle and many times, wounding him and thus provoking an attack. What could have started as bear approaching a human to satisfy his curiosity would end with an enraged bear with two or three bullets lodged in his hide and fury aimed at the person who shot him. Through these sorts of encounters, the grizzly earned his reputation for being ferocious.

Who can blame the early explorers and settlers for being fearful of the great grizzly? Many believed that they had better shoot first before the beast deprived them of their livestock or their own lives. The pioneers acted defensively, not believing that man and grizzly could ever co-exist.

The same attitude is shared today by many, while others have learned to accept the grizzly's presence and have even learned to enjoy living and sharing the land with him. Bud Sheff is such a man. He has spent fifty years ranching at the foot of the Mission Mountains in western Montana, an area which has always been prime grizzly habitat. He says that in all his years of ranching in the Missions, he may have lost two or three calves to grizzlies, but even these losses, he speculates, could have come from local black bears, who have proven more troublesome. Bud recalls many times in the past when grizzlies, cattle, and horses grazed in the pasture near his barn. The grizzlies even ignored the newborn calves.

When asked if he ever had any close calls with the grizzly, he said, "Sure, there were times we had to run them out of our front yard, but we never had any serious trouble," adding, "I raised seven kids here and didn't feed any to the bears."

Bud Sheff, along with many others, are witnesses that man and grizzly can co-exist. Canadian rancher Andy Russell is another example. Russell's Book, *Grizzly Country,* describes how Russell and his children coexisted with grizzlies at the foot of the Canadian Rockies. These individuals learned that if they followed a few safety precautions, the danger of surprise encounters were kept to a minimum.

No one has ever come up with a one hundred percent, fool-proof way to avoid danger when facing the grizzly. The many variables make it difficult, and each bear is an individual unto himself. There are, however, some general rules to follow that will help avoid a conflict between man and bear.

First, it should be remembered that when a grizzly meets a human, the bear will often turn and run. When the bear does approach a person, it can be motivated by curiosity or a desire to identify the creature. In this case, it is advisable to wave your arms and shout; remain calm, try not to panic, and don't run. When the bear stops, back up or step aside to give the bear room to get around you.

If the grizzly is at close range when he stops, talk to him. Never squat or kneel, because this can be interpreted by the bear as submissive behavior. Again, slowly back off and give the grizzly room. If the bear follows you, growling or snapping his teeth, he could be an abnormally hostile specimen; if there is a tree close by, try to climb it, dropping things behind you to distract the animal (remember that a determined grizzly can climb trees, as well, using the limbs to pull himself up). If there is no tree or other refuge close by, continue to slowly back away. Only if the grizzly charges at close range should you resort to lying on the ground in a fetal position, with hands clasped behind your neck to protect that vulnerable area from bites. When in this position, do not talk, yell, or move. The odds that the bear will abandon the confrontation are still in your favor.

People should be prepared before going into grizzly country. Chuck Jonkel's booklet, *How to Live in Bear Country,* and Steve Herrero's book, *Bear Attacks: Their Causes and Avoidance,* are excellent sources of detailed information with life-saving value.

Will the Grizzly Survive?

No one today can definitely state how far the grizzlies ranged on this continent. Based on reports from early white explorers, it is known grizzlies were observed almost to Hudson Bay, with the eastern limits running south through Saskatchewan, the Great Plains, North and South Dakota, Nebraska, and continuing south into central Mexico. The range included most of the area west of this line all the way to the Pacific Ocean and extended north to the Arctic tundra. This area probably contained a grizzly population that numbered fifty to one hundred thousand.

When snow begins to accumulate and food becomes less plentiful, the grizzly heads for its winter den.

Before the coming of the white man, the grizzly had little to fear in his wilderness domain. Indians occasionally hunted the grizzly, but considering the primitive weapons used, it is doubtful that they enjoyed great success. In fact, if one were able to tally up the grizzly losses in one column and the Indian losses in the other, I would surmise that the Indian would come out with the larger loss total.

It wasn't until the appearance of the explorers and their muskets that the balance began tipping against the grizzly. Armed with this weapon, and later, the more advanced repeating rifle, the white man eliminated the great bear from most of its southern range. The grizzly was hunted and trapped with a vengeance. Sheep and cattle ranchers shot

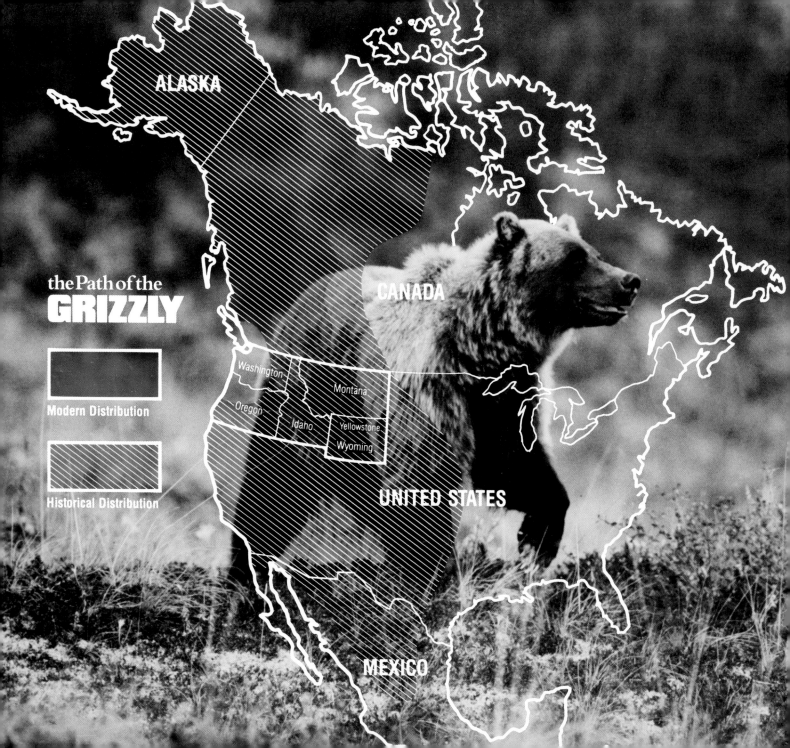

the Path of the
GRIZZLY

Modern Distribution

Historical Distribution

ALASKA

CANADA

Washington

Montana

Oregon

Idaho

Yellowstone

Wyoming

UNITED STATES

MEXICO

grizzlies on sight, whether the bear was killing livestock or not. The motivation was simple: fear. What the early settlers feared they eliminated, whether it be grizzlies, wolves, or Indians.

Although the grizzly still survives in fairly sizeable numbers in Alaska and western Canada, the same cannot be said for the continental United States. Here, the grizzly has been reduced to a few scattered remnants—the total of which may fall short of eight hundred grizzlies, less than one to two percent of former numbers.

Other than a few small populations in northern Washington, Idaho, and northwestern Montana, the vast majority are concentrated in two areas. The largest is in Montana; called the Northern Continental Divide Ecosystem, it contains an estimated four hundred-fifty to six hundred-fifty grizzlies. This area includes Glacier National Park on the Canadian border and extends south to Lincoln along Highway 200. It is bordered on the western boundary by the Mission Mountains, and its eastern limits stretch onto the Great Plains.

The other area, known as the Yellowstone Ecosystem, supports less than two hundred grizzlies. It includes Yellowstone and Grand Teton national parks and the adjacent national forest land in Montana, Wyoming, and Idaho.

The question now is how long can these remaining grizzlies survive under increasing pressure from an expanding human population that demands more and more from shrinking resources. Timber harvesting, energy development, mining, new roads, land developments, and subdivisions are some of the activities that gradually chip away at the grizzlies' "wilderness habitat"—in some cases right up the boundaries of Yellowstone and Glacier national parks.

Most of those responsible for saving the grizzly believe that the key to his survival is stopping the destruction of his habitat. Chuck Jonkel, a world-renowned bear biologist and head of the Border Grizzly Project, states, "Habitat is the key to grizzly survival. As long as we have wild areas for him to live, we will have the grizzly."

Unfortunately, not everyone is concerned with the plight of the grizzly. Some think that we can't afford the grizzly. They view him as a stumbling block to timber and energy interests who would like to open up more federal land for their use. Since the grizzly was declared a threatened species in 1975 under the Endangered Species Act, there have been more restrictions on activities that might jeopardize his recovery. For some—those who make their living in the forests of Montana—the grizzly is a major problem. Considering that many of these areas are already economically depressed, it is understandable that there might be local apathy towards the bear's plight.

Habitat loss isn't the only problem facing the grizzly. As one outspoken critic put it, "All the

Glacier National Park, Montana—grizzly country

habitat in the world won't do us any good if all we can put in it are dead grizzlies." Some biologists fear that the grizzly's slow reproductive rate is not keeping up with mortalities, and that the bear is losing ground as a result.

Each year grizzlies die from a variety of causes. Some are killed in control actions to eliminate problem bears. Others are lost to research accidents, such as drug overdoses, or in relocation. A few are lost to poachers. Ranchers (particularly sheep ranchers) are prone to shooting grizzlies who wander anywhere near their livestock. Each year, black-bear hunters kill a few grizzlies by mistake. The most controversial killing of grizzlies takes place along the northern Continental Divide in Montana. As of this time, Montana is the only state outside of Alaska that has a legal hunting season; up until 1985, a total of twenty-five grizzlies could be taken out of the Northern Continental Divide Ecosystem. This total represented kills from all sources, including control actions, illegal kills, accidents, etc. When twenty-five mortalities occurred, the hunting season ended.

A number of conservation organizations have been against this hunt for some time. They feel that since the Montana Fish, Wildlife & Parks Department doesn't know for sure how many grizzlies there are in this ecosystem or whether the population is increasing, decreasing, or stable, hunting should not be allowed. The state's position is that there is a surplus of grizzlies and that these should

be hunted. In 1985, the Montana Fish, Wildlife & Parks Department did reduce the quota to fifteen grizzlies.

Biologists and conservationists seem divided on the hunting issue. Some say that if bears are hunted they retain their fear of man, which lessens the possibility of conflicts. Others disagree, stating that since we don't know how many grizzlies there are we shouldn't assume there are enough to hunt. Also, they ask, how do dead grizzlies learn to fear man?

What lies ahead for the grizzly? Is there a place for him in our society? Yes, but not a very big one.

In July 1985, the Montana Fish, Wildlife & Parks Department wrote letters to fifteen western states and three Canadian provinces and two territories, all of which at one time had grizzly populations, asking if they would take up to twenty-five relocated grizzles a year. With the exception of the Canadian province of British Columbia, which expressed mild interest in transplanting grizzlies to a few select areas, all declined the offer. Many people want grizzlies but only as long as they remain in Montana, Canada, or Alaska.

It seems clear that it is very unlikely that the grizzly will ever expand his range beyond what it is now. Perhaps the goal should be to concentrate on saving the grizzlies we have left.

Some people, however, question the need for the grizzly. They argue that his disappearance would not affect the balance of nature. They say that the mountains would be safer without his supposedly ferocious presence. They ask what purpose he possibly serves. Others offer answers to these questions.

A rancher, Len Sargent, who has been raising cattle for twenty five years just north of Yellowstone National Park in prime grizzly habitat, had this to say about the importance of the bear, "In the old days, canaries were put in coal mines to serve as an alarm system for the build-up of poisonous gas. If the canary died, the miners knew that something was wrong. Well, the grizzly serves a similar purpose. As he is eliminated from our remaining wildlands, it is a warning to us that maybe we aren't doing something right. The grizzly, in effect, is serving as a large canary to our wilderness."

Despite the magnitude of the problems facing the grizzly, there are concerted efforts being made to reduce his losses and aid his recovery. Intensive research is being conducted by a number of organizations and government agencies. The Yellowstone Interagency Grizzly Bear Study Team, with representatives from the National Park Service; U.S. Fish & Wildlife Service; Forest Service; and fish and game departments of Montana, Wyoming, and Idaho, under biologist Dick Knight, is working in the Yellowstone Ecosystem. The Border Grizzly Project, headed by Chuck Jonkel, is studying grizzlies in the northern Rockies and also working on aversive-conditioning techniques that may help in reducing bear-man conflicts.

The mapping of large areas of grizzly habitat using satellite imagery is being developed by John Craighead, Director of the Wildlife-Wildlands Institute, well-known for his research on grizzlies. He is working on a way to satellite-track grizzlies, which could be very useful in determining areas critical to the bear's survival.

In addition to these research projects, separate studies by state and federal agencies are in process, and there are a few specific management policies being instituted to cut down on bear mortalities.

More effort is being made by various agencies to strengthen law enforcement and reduce poaching. Along with this, the National Audubon Society offers a $15,000 reward for information leading to the arrest and conviction of anyone illegally killing a grizzly bear.

There are areas where black bear hunting is restricted to reduce grizzly losses due to mistaken identity by hunters.

Efforts are being made to reduce the number of sheep-grazing allotments on federal land, to reduce conflicts there.

Proper disposal of garbage, by individuals as well as entire communities, is being encouraged to avoid the necessity of killing bears that become addicted to this food source.

An early snowstorm frosts this grizzly's coat with ice crystals.

The Great Bear Foundation, under the direction of president Lance Olsen, has initiated a compensation program for ranchers who have suffered livestock losses to grizzlies on private land. Two payments were made this year to ranchers on the Rocky Mountain Front in Montana. It is hoped that this program will assist in creating a better attitude among ranchers toward the grizzly.

These, as well as others, are positive steps being implemented to save the grizzly. Thanks to a few dedicated individuals who work with limited budgets, and quite often with little pay, there remains some hope for the great bear.

Now we must convince the general public that the grizzly is worth saving.

For, it would seem, in the final analysis, the greatest single influence on the survival of the grizzly rests in the hands of public opinion and education. This is not only true for the destiny of the grizzly, but all of nature's creations who rely on American wilderness resources for their continued survival.

The grizzly will survive as long as there is a place for him and as long as man lets him survive. It is man who controls the destiny of this land and its resources, and so it is man who controls the living things supported by the land. The great and most powerful animal on the continent is still, ironically, only as powerful as he is allowed to be.

Ultimately, you and I have the final say on the continued existence of this great animal, the grizzly.

Its heavy coat riffled by a strong autumn wind, a grizzly faces man, his most potent enemy.

The Yellowstone Association

for Natural Science, History & Education, Inc.

What is the Yellowstone Association?

The Yellowstone Association is a non-profit, tax-exempt organization, whose purpose is to support historic, educational, and scientific programs related to Yellowstone Park. The Association generates funds to meet this goal in two ways: through the sale of interpretive books, magazines and videos in this and other Yellowstone visitor centers and through our contributing membership program.

What types of things will my membership be used for?

The Yellowstone Association provides financial support to educational programs here in Yellowstone. For example, the Association purchases audiovisual and computer equipment for use by the ranger naturalists in presenting programs and publications for visitors, helps fund wayside exhibits, staffs the park library and obtains new reference materials for use by the park staff and the visiting public and provides the trail brochures (over 575,000 annually) which are available at many park locations. Since its inception, the Yellowstone Association has provided aid to Yellowstone Park in excess of $1,250,000 and continues to be an important part of providing interpretive programs to educate visitors about this magnificent park and its preservation.

YA also sponsors the Yellowstone Institute, an outstanding program of summer field classes given throughout Yellowstone, with headquarters in the beautiful Lamar Valley.

This is a partial listing of nonprofit organizations that are working in many different ways toward the preservation of the grizzly and his habitat.

Your support would be appreciated.

GREAT BEAR FOUNDATION

Dedicated to the conservation of all wild bears (with special emphasis on the grizzly bear) in a wild habitat. The foundation also publishes a quarterly newspaper, *Bear News.*

P.O. Box 2699
Missoula, Montana 59806

THE GREATER YELLOWSTONE COALITION

Its goal is a commitment to the preservation of a healthy Yellowstone ecosystem. A special emphasis is put on the grizzly because it is a symbol and indicator of the health of the ecosystem.

P.O. Box 1874
40 East Main Street
Bozeman, Montana 59715

THE NATURE CONSERVANCY

Its goal is to identify and protect (primarily through land acquisitions) habitat that is critical to rare and endangered species. The Conservancy owns an eleven-thousand acre preserve in the Rocky Mountain Front in Montana called Pine Butte Swamp—a diverse area of foothill prairie and spring-fed wetlands purchased primarily to protect the grizzly.

Big Sky Field Office
P.O Box 258
Helena, Montana 59624

WILDLIFE-WILDLANDS INSTITUTE

Dedicated to solving ecological problems through intensive, long-term research. A lot of this research has been directed toward the grizzly, including the use of satellite imagery to map grizzly habitat.

5200 Upper Miller Creek Road
Missoula, Montana 59803

Alan Carey is a professional wildlife photographer whose work has appeared in such publications as *National Wildlife, Smithsonian,* and *National Geographic World.* His love of wildlife and his desire to photograph America's animals and birds in their natural habitats have taken him from the Florida Everglades to the frozen Alaskan tundra. He lives with his wife and children in Montana.